Welcome my friend, your jour

This colouring book was created with YOU in mind – both as a tool for stress re in your day to day life. Colouring, drawing, or simply gazing at a mandala can be a very meditative process. For some, it can also offer a healing element. After experiencing these healing properties for myself, helping others to discover the power of mandalas has become a passion of mine. With that in mind, and with the help of this book, I hope you enjoy your own mandala journey.

Intentions

An Intention is an idea, phrase, or thought on which you'd like to focus or bring attention to in your everyday life. Each mandala in this book has been created with a specific intention that can be found on the back side of that page. You can use the intention provided, or you have the freedom of choosing a unique intention that speaks to you.

I recommend trying a simple breathing exercise before you begin colouring, as they are an amazing way to help focus your intention in the centre of your mind. Make sure you are sitting comfortably in your seat then relax your shoulders and close your eyes. Breathe in for four counts through your nose, and out for four counts through your mouth. Do this four times. Think about your intention as you inhale, and imagine the stresses of your day receding as you exhale.

Colour

I highly encourage you to let go and allow your colour choices to be influenced by your intention. Try to choose colours that feel right without concerning yourself about whether your choices go together. This journey is about bringing your intention to focus, so take notice of how that intention affects your colour choices.

When you are satisfied with your mandala, you might choose to remove the page from this book and frame the piece in order to remind you of your intention or to use it in meditation (find instructions on how to meditate on your mandala on the back of this book).

Remember there are no rules to this process, and there should be no predetermined outcomes. It's perfectly OK to leave a mandala black and white, and frame it as is, if that's how you feel it should be. You may also feel free to give a mandala to a friend you think will appreciate its intention for them to keep or colour.

Other Tips

Ambiance is important – bring a sense of calm to your space with candles, incense, and music. Slip into your comfy clothes. Grab your favourite drink. Carve out some time for yourself and get into your Zen. Whether it's for ten minutes or ten hours, make time for yourself to colour with intention, and notice a refreshing change in your perspective.

Sending you much love and positive vibes.

To frame your mandala

All of the pages in this book have been customized to fit a standard size 8" x 10" frame. The images will be perfectly centred horizontally as long as you cut the page out .5" away from the spine of the book along the dotted line on the back of the mandala. To centre the page vertically, cut .5" from both the top and bottom of the page.

I am Love

Peace exists in my heart

Strength

I live a life of passion

Wisdom

Courage

Forgiveness

Good Karma

Magic

Everything that has happened
in my life, whether positive or negative,
makes me who I am today,
and I am beautiful

Find light in the dark

Softly & gracefully dancing through life

I have the strength to
make difficult decisions

I embrace change

Remain light and airy
when life becomes heavy

I am confident in who I am
and what I believe in

Stand my ground

I accept the things I cannot change

Willpower

Live to my fullest potential

Circle of Life

Perfectly imperfect

Beautiful soul

Gratitude

My intentions are powerful

Made in the USA
Columbia, SC
02 October 2018